AF599276

Baby Animals in the Wild!

Raccoon Cubs in the Wild

by Katie Chanez

Ideas for Parents and Teachers

Bullfrog Books let children practice reading informational text at the earliest reading levels. Repetition, familiar words, and photo labels support early readers.

Before Reading

- Discuss the cover photo. What does it tell them?
- Look at the picture glossary together. Read and discuss the words.

Read the Book

- "Walk" through the book and look at the photos. Let the child ask questions. Point out the photo labels.
- Read the book to the child, or have him or her read independently.

After Reading

- Prompt the child to think more. Ask: Raccoon cubs live in a den. Can you name other animals that live in dens?

Bullfrog Books are published by Jump!
5357 Penn Avenue South
Minneapolis, MN 55419
www.jumplibrary.com

Library of Congress Cataloging-in-Publication Data

Names: Chanez, Katie, author.
Title: Raccoon cubs in the wild / by Katie Chanez.
Description: Minneapolis, MN: Jump!, Inc., [2024]
Series: Baby animals in the wild! | Includes index.
Audience: Ages 5–8
Identifiers: LCCN 2022044316 (print)
LCCN 2022044317 (ebook)
ISBN 9798885244121 (hardcover)
ISBN 9798885244138 (paperback)
ISBN 9798885244145 (ebook)
Subjects: LCSH: Raccoon—Infancy—Juvenile literature.
Classification: LCC QL737.C26 C43 2024 (print)
LCC QL737.C26 (ebook)
DDC 599.76/32—dc23/eng/20220920
LC record available at https://lccn.loc.gov/2022044316
LC ebook record available at https://lccn.loc.gov/2022044317

Editor: Eliza Leahy
Designer: Molly Ballanger

Photo Credits: Tyler Plum/Shutterstock, cover; Eric Isselee/Shutterstock, 1, 3 (raccoon); Sonsedska Yuliia/Shutterstock, 3 (cub), 8, 23br, 24; Farzad Darabi/Shutterstock, 4; Design Pics/SuperStock, 5, 23tl; Morales/age fotostock/SuperStock, 6–7, 23tr; Agnieszka Bacal/Shutterstock, 9; skhoward/iStock, 10–11, 23bl; marcophotos/iStock, 12–13; Suzi Eszterhas/Minden Pictures/SuperStock, 14–15; Warren Metcalf/Shutterstock, 16; Design Pics Inc/Alamy, 17; Rinus Baak/Dreamstime, 18–19; Rolf Nussbaumer Photography/Alamy, 20–21; Anton Vierietin/Shutterstock, 22.

Printed in the United States of America at Corporate Graphics in North Mankato, Minnesota.

Table of Contents

Ringed Tail

A raccoon mom climbs a tree.

Why?

Her den is inside.

Her cubs are in it.

The cubs are safe in the den.

They grow.

A cub has a mask.

It has a fluffy tail.
Its tail has rings.
ring

The cubs explore.
They climb trees.

They play!

They find eggs to eat.

How?

Mom shows them!

egg

The cubs learn to fish.

He got one!

The cubs grow up.

They stay with Mom through winter.

Brr!

crayfish

In spring, they go off on their own.

They find many foods to eat.

Yum!

Parts of a Raccoon Cub

What are the parts of a raccoon cub? Take a look!

Picture Glossary

cubs
Baby raccoons.

den
The home of a wild animal.

explore
To travel and look around in order to discover things.

mask
A covering for the face to hide, protect, or disguise it.

Index

To Learn More

Finding more information is as easy as 1, 2, 3.

1. Go to www.factsurfer.com
2. Enter "raccooncubs" into the search box.
3. Choose your book to see a list of websites.